Living in a Desert

By Allan Fowler

Consultant
Linda Cornwell, Coordinator of School Quality
and Professional Improvement
Indiana State Teachers Association

Children's Press®
A Division of Grolier Publishing
New York   London   Hong Kong   Sydney
Danbury, Connecticut

Designer: Herman Adler Design Group

Library of Congress Cataloging-in-Publication Data

Fowler, Allan.
    Living in a desert / by Allan Fowler; consultant, Linda Cornwell.
        p. cm. — (Rookie read-about geography)
    Includes index.
    Summary: Discusses people who live in desert areas of the world
and how it affects their lives.
    ISBN: 0-516-21560-4 (lib. bdg.)   0-516-27049-4 (pbk.)
    1. Desert people Juvenile literature. 2. Deserts Juvenile literature.
3. Desert ecology Juvenile literature. [1. Desert people. 2. Deserts.
3. Desert ecology. 4. Ecology.] I. Title.
II. Series.
GN390.F68   2000
577.54—dc21   99-14945
                                                              CIP

A desert is a dry, sandy area. Few plants grow in a desert because there is little rainfall.

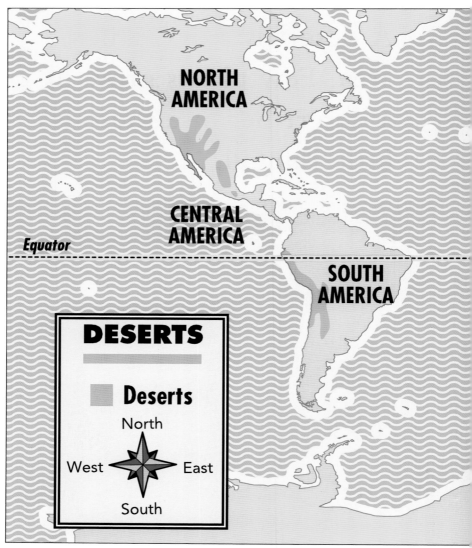

This map shows where the deserts of the world are located.

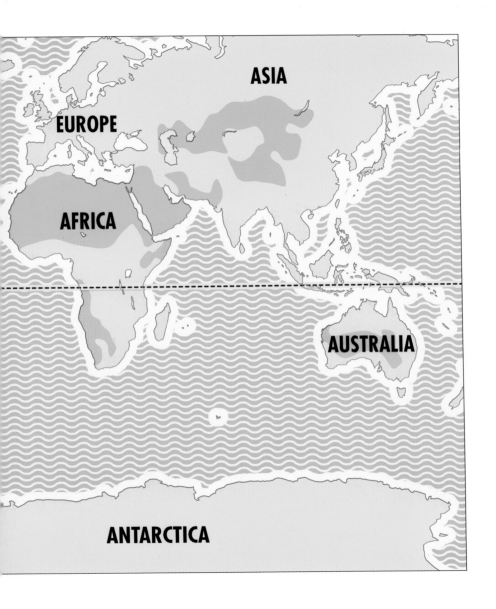

ASIA

EUROPE

AFRICA

AUSTRALIA

ANTARCTICA

Desert town in Algeria, a country in Africa

Not many people live in the world's deserts. But some people do call the desert home.

People called bedouins
(BE-duh-wuhnz) live
in the Sahara and
Arabian deserts.

Bedouin family

Bedouins often move from place to place. They look for areas with enough grass for their sheep and goats to eat.

Bedouins with a flock of goats and sheep

Bedouin tents

Their homes are tents
made of cloth.

Bedouins riding camels

Most bedouins do not drive cars or trucks because there are few roads in the desert. They ride horses or camels.

These people live in
the Gobi Desert of Asia.
Like the bedouins, they
raise sheep and goats.

An adobe house

Many people who live
in the deserts of North
America build homes of
adobe (uh-DOH-bee).

Adobe is a kind of brick
made of clay mixed with
straw. It is dried in the sun
until it hardens.

Deserts can be very hot during the day, and very cold at night.

Many desert people in Africa and Asia stay comfortable by wearing a long, loose robe. Most of the robes are made of wool. Some have an attached hood.

This man lives in the desert in Egypt, a country in Africa.

Air-conditioned homes in the desert near Las Vegas, Nevada

Many people who live in cities or towns near deserts have air conditioning to keep them cool.

Some people who live
in or near the desert
work in mines.

Many deserts are rich
in minerals such as salt.

Oil and natural gas
lie under some deserts,
as well.

Workers in a South American salt mine

This is the Sahara Desert.
It is the world's largest
desert and lies in
northern Africa.

Farmers can now grow crops in the Sahara and other deserts.

Pipes and ditches carry water from faraway rivers or lakes. This is called irrigation (ihr-uh-GAY-shun).

This desert farmer waters his crops from an irrigation ditch.

Life in the desert can be hard. That is why few people live in the world's deserts.

But the people who do live in them have found ways to make life there work.

Words You Know

adobe

bedouins

desert

irrigation

mine

robe

31

Index

About the Author

Allan Fowler is a freelance writer with a background in advertising.
Born in New York, he now lives in Chicago and enjoys traveling.

Photo Credits

©: BBC Natural History Unit: 3, 31 top left (Jeff Foott), 15 (Martha Holmes);
Ben Klaffke: 16, 30 top; Panos Pictures: 27, 31 top right (Jeremy Hartley), 23, 31
bottom left (Jeremy Horner), 19, 31 bottom right (G. Mansfield); Photo
Researchers: 11 (Laura Zito); The Image Works: 28 (Michael Justice), 20 (J.
Marshall), 9, 30 bottom (N. Schiller), 10 (Topham); Tony Stone Images: cover
(Sylvain Grandadam); Victor Englebert: 6, 12, 24.

Map by Joe LeMonnier.